C000140287

Portmanteau A–Z

# Portmanteau A–Z
## An Alphabet of Portmanteau Words

Rebecca May

*For Tessa, Tony and Sam*

'Twas brillig, and the slithy toves
Did gyre and gimble in the wabe:
All mimsy were the borogoves,
And the mome raths outgrabe.

Lewis Carroll, 'Jabberwocky', in *Through the
Looking-Glass, and What Alice Found There*, 1871

A portmanteau word (also known as a blend) is a word that fuses the sounds and combines the meanings of two or more other words. A portmanteau – itself a blend of the French words *porter* ('to carry') and *manteau* ('mantle') – is a leather case or trunk that opens in two equal parts. The term 'portmanteau word' was coined by Lewis Carroll in his novel *Through the Looking-Glass, and What Alice Found There* (1871). When Alice asks Humpty Dumpty the meaning of the word 'slithy' in the poem 'Jabberwocky', he replies, 'Well, "*slithy*" means "lithe and slimy." … You see it's like a portmanteau – there are two meanings packed up into one word.'

Some of Carroll's word inventions in 'Jabberwocky' have become part of our language and have worked their way into the *Oxford English Dictionary*: for example, 'chortle' (from *chuckle* + *snort*) and 'galumph' (from *gallop* + *triumph*; see page 24).

This volume of words derives from a delight in the English language and its use in the poetry of Lewis Carroll, Edward Lear and, more recently, Michael Rosen. When it came to choosing words for inclusion, I discovered that it's possible to harbour strong feelings about the sound of a word entirely divorced from its meaning. The feel of a word as it comes out of the mouth or the shape the face must make in order to pronounce a word may equally induce pleasure or repulsion. This book is devoted to our very physical and immediate relationship with the sound and usage of words. The most interesting portmanteau words seem to be those that pop out spontaneously, squeezing the most effective definition from a tangle of words. This technique is best described by Carroll himself in the preface to his epic nonsense poem *The Hunting of the Snark* (1876):

... take the two words 'fuming' and 'furious.' Make up your mind that you will say both words, but leave it unsettled which you will say first. Now open your mouth and speak. If your thoughts incline ever so little towards 'fuming,' you will say 'fuming-furious'; if they turn, by even a hair's breadth, towards 'furious,' you will say 'furious-fuming'; but if you have that rarest of gifts, a perfectly balanced mind, you will say 'fruminous.'

# anticipointment

/anˌtɪsɪˈpɔɪntmənt/ *n.*

the moment when a prolonged period of
suspense concludes with unfortunate results.
[ANTICI(PATION) + (DISAP)POINTMENT]

33　　　9

# bleen

/bliːn/ *adj.*

the colour created by mixing together the
colours blue and green.
[BL(UE) + (GR)EEN]

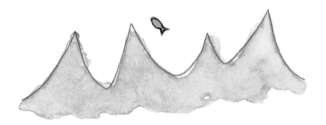

# cankle

/ˈkaŋk(ə)l/ *n.*

the part of the leg where the ankle should be,
but where the calf and foot appear to merge as
a result of genetics or a lack of circulation.
[c(ALF) + ANKLE]

# digerati

/ˌdɪdʒəˈrɑːti/ *pl. n.*

the influential members of the computer
industry and on-line communities, or those with
an in-depth knowledge of digital technology.
[DIG(ITAL) + (LIT)ERATI]

# ecotage

/ˈiːkəʊtɑːʒ/ *n.*

an act of vandalism or violence, carried out in
the name of environmental protection.
[ECO + (SABO)TAGE]

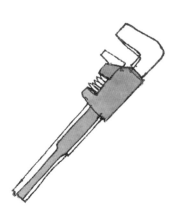

# Frankenfood

/ˈfraŋk(ə)nfuːd/ *n.*

genetically modified foodstuffs.
[FRANKEN(STEIN) + FOOD]

# galumph

/gəˈlʌmf/ *v.*

to prance triumphantly; to move
heavily and clumsily.
[GAL(LOP) + (TRI)UMPH]

# hangry

/ˈhaŋgri/ *adj.*

feeling emotionally and physically distressed
after a long period without food – sufferers are
prone to become tearful and irrational.
[H(UNGRY) + ANGRY]

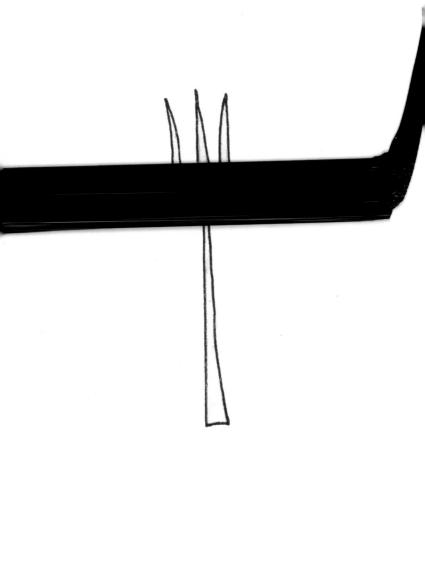

# infomercial

/ˌɪnfə(ʊ)ˈməːʃ(ə)l/ *n.*

an extended commercial, made to resemble a
television programme, that informs or instructs.
[INFO(RMATION) + (COM)MERCIAL]

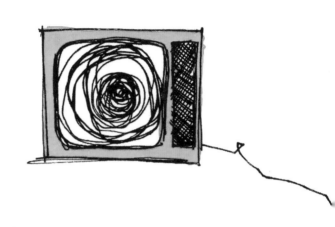

# jipple

/ˈdʒɪp(ə)l/ *n.*

a painful condition caused by the continuous
chafing of clothing against nipples during
jogging or other exercise.
[J(OG) + (N)IPPLE]

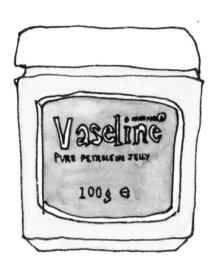

# Kripkenstein

/ˈkrɪpk(ə)nstʌɪn/ *n.*

the philosopher Saul Kripke's controversial
interpretation of Ludwig Wittgenstein's
*Philosophical Investigations* (1953), as presented
in Kripke's book *Wittgenstein on Rules and
Private Language* (1982).
[KRIPKE + (WITTGE)NSTEIN]

# WITTGENSTEIN
## ON RULES
## AND PRIVATE
## LANGUAGE

### BY
### SAUL KRIPKE

# liger

/ˈlʌɪɡə/ *n.*

the offspring of a male lion and a tigress, 'bred
for its skills in magic' according to the fictional
character Napoleon Dynamite.
[L(ION) + (T)IGER]

# mimsy

/ˈmɪmzi/ *adj.*

wretchedly unhappy; weak, affected and
lacking life.
[MI(SERABLE) + (FLI)MSY]

# navaid

/ˈnaveɪd/ *n.*

a navigational aid or device.
[NAV(IGATIONAL) + AID]

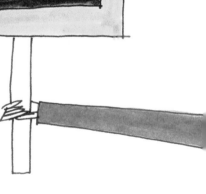

# Oxbridge

/ˈɒksbrɪdʒ/ *n.*

a reference to the universities of both Oxford and Cambridge, and the characteristics of these two institutions as privileged centres of learning. [OX(FORD) + (CAM)BRIDGE]

# politricks

/ˈpɒlɪtrɪks/ *pl. n.*

the lies and spin in which politicians engage for
party benefit.
[POLI(TICS) + TRICKS]

# quasar

/ˈkweɪzɑː/ *n.*

an extremely distant, energetic and luminous
celestial object, starlike in appearance.
[QUAS(I-STELLAR) + (ST)AR]

# ruckus

/ˈrʌkəs/ *n.*

an unpleasant commotion, row or disturbance.
[RUC(TION) + (RUMP)US]

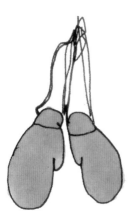

# stumblesharf

/ˈstʌmb(ə)lʃɑːf/ *n.*

the stubbly hair that sprouts within minutes of
using a cheap disposable razor, appearing on
legs, in armpits and on various other body parts.
[STUMBLE + STU(B)BLE + SHAR(P)]

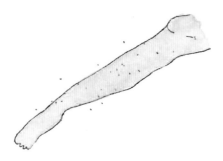

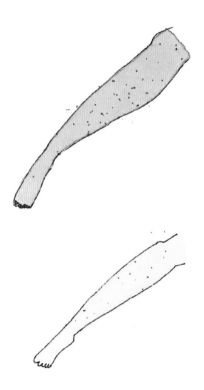

# tinkelmurk

/ˈtɪŋk(ə)lməːk/ *v.*

to urinate in an audibly controlled or
disguised fashion.
[TINK(LE) + M(EE)K + (DEM)UR(E)]

# uffish

/ˈʌfɪʃ/ *adj.*

'a state of mind when the voice is gruffish,
the manner roughish, and the temper huffish',
according to Lewis Carroll in a letter to his
friend Maud Standen in 1877.
[(GR)UFFISH + (ROUGH)ISH + (H)UFFISH]

# vog

/vɒg/ *n.*

the air pollution caused by volcanic gases
reacting with oxygen, moisture and sunlight.
[v(olcanic) + (f)og]

# wholphin

/ˈwɒlfɪn/ *n.*

the offspring of a male false killer whale and
a female Atlantic bottlenose dolphin.
[WH(ALE) + (D)OLPHIN]

# xrunkopy

/zrʌŋˈkɒpi/ *v.*

to commit mischievous behaviour at an office party (the term originates from the alcohol-induced photocopying of one's bottom).
[x(EROX) + (D)RUNK + (PHOTOC)OPY]

# youthanasia

/ˌjuːθəˈneɪzɪə/ *n.*

the act of a society euthanizing its youth, as
coined by the thrash-metal band Megadeth for
the title of their 1994 album.
[YOUTH + (EUTH)ANASIA]

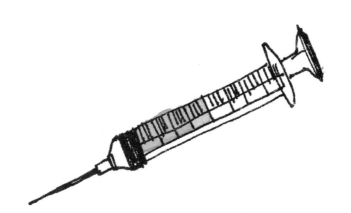

## zorse

/zɔːs/ *n.*

the offspring of a zebra stallion and
a horse mare.
[z(EBRA) + (H)ORSE]